READABOUT

Texture

This edition 2003

Franklin Watts
96 Leonard Street
London EC2A 4XD

Franklin Watts Australia
45-51 Huntley Street
Alexandria
NSW 2015

Editor: Ambreen Husain
Design: K and Co

Additional Photographs:
Royal National Institute for the Blind p. 30

A CIP catalogue record for this book is available
from the British Library.

ISBN 0 7496 5274 8

Printed in Hong Kong

READABOUT
Texture

Text: Henry Pluckrose
Photography: Chris Fairclough

W
FRANKLIN WATTS
LONDON·SYDNEY

Texture is a word
which explains
how things feel
when we touch them.
These stones have
sharp, spiky edges.
When you touch them
they feel hard and rough.

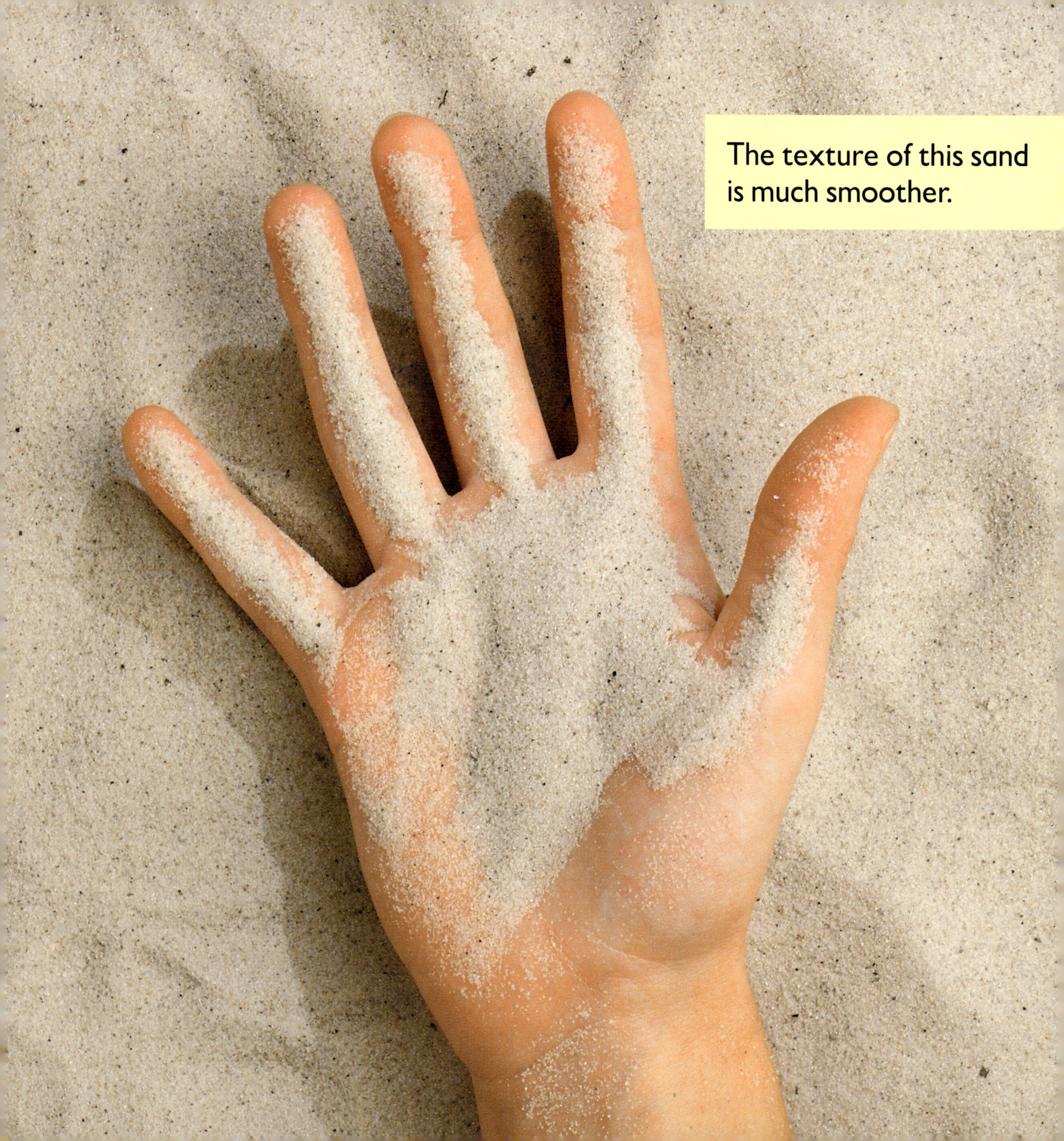

The texture of this sand
is much smoother.

We can see textures
in nature...
in the veins of leaves,
on the bark of trees,
on the stems of
thistles,
in feathers.

Look at these fruits.
How would you describe
the texture of their skins?

Wood has texture.
Some trees have smooth bark.
Some bark is deeply grained
or lightly lined.

When a tree is cut down you can see a new texture, the rings within the trunk.

Textures change.
Rough logs,
splintery planks...

planed,
smoothed,
become furniture.

One material can have different textures. The wool on the sheep has a different texture to knitting wool, woollen blankets, woollen clothes.

Soaps...
powdery,
liquid,
smooth and oily.

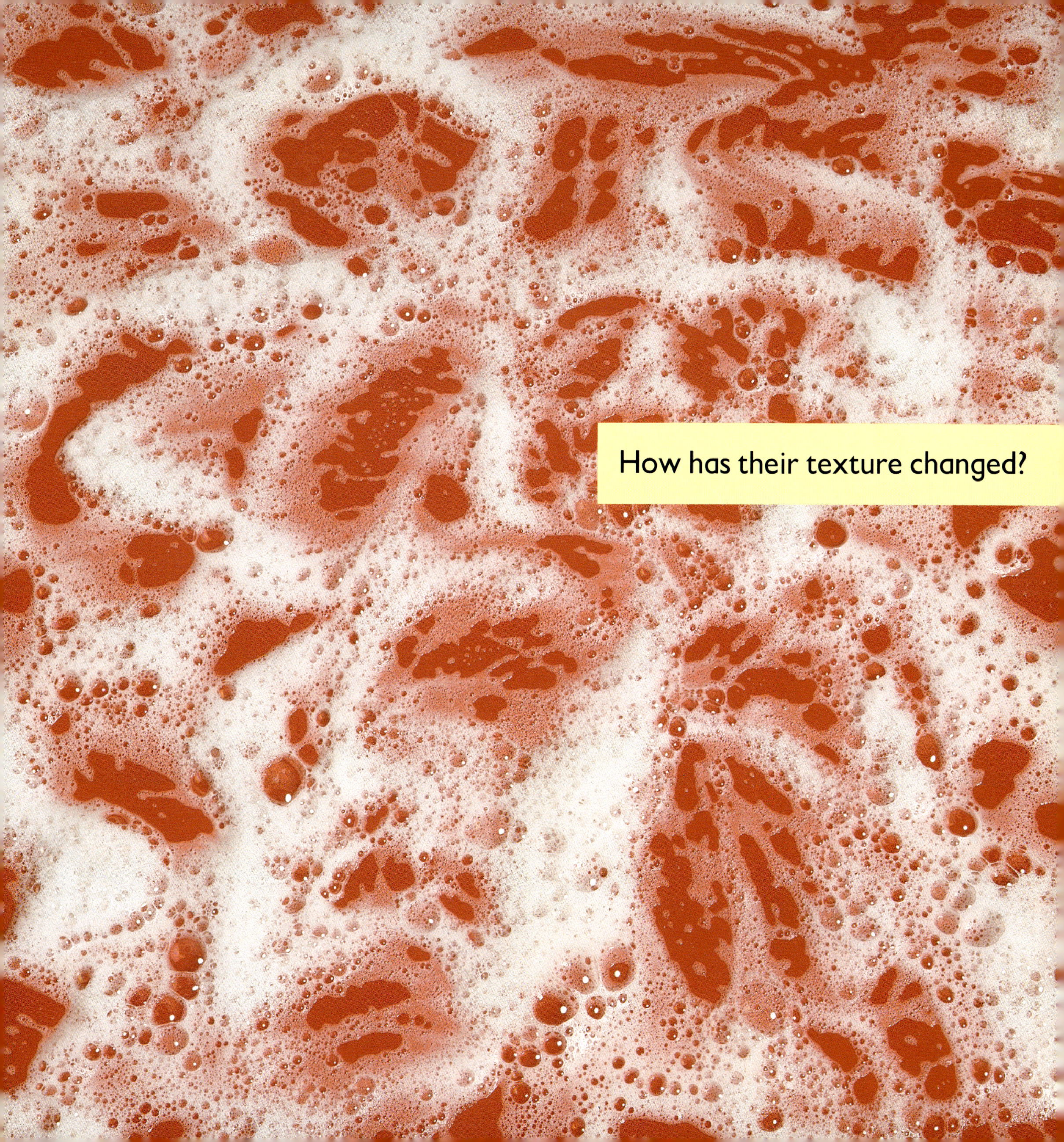

How has their texture changed?

Textures are all around us.
Paper like this
looks good on a wall…
but you could not use it
to write on.

Stones arranged like these
make a pretty pattern…
but you could not use them
for a road.

Everything has a texture...
hair, wool, scale, shell.

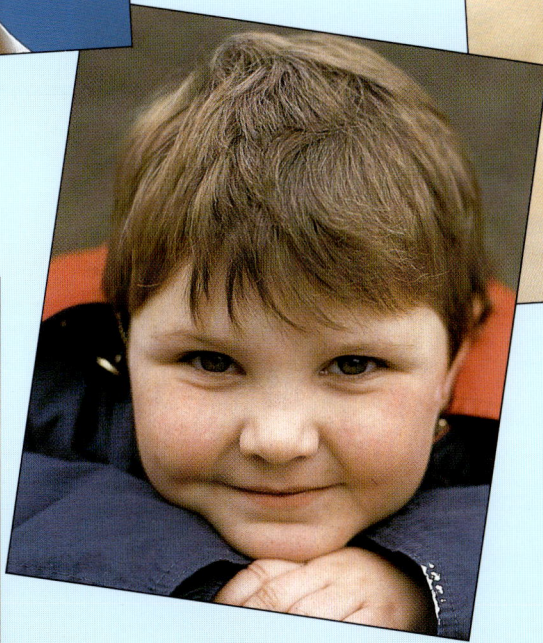

Does your skin have a texture?
Does your hair have the same
texture as your friend's?

Our eyes give us information
about the texture of things
but we need to touch them too.
The surface of the towel
looks rough but it will
feel soft against the skin.
Sand paper has a rough
surface too,
but you would never dry
your face on it!

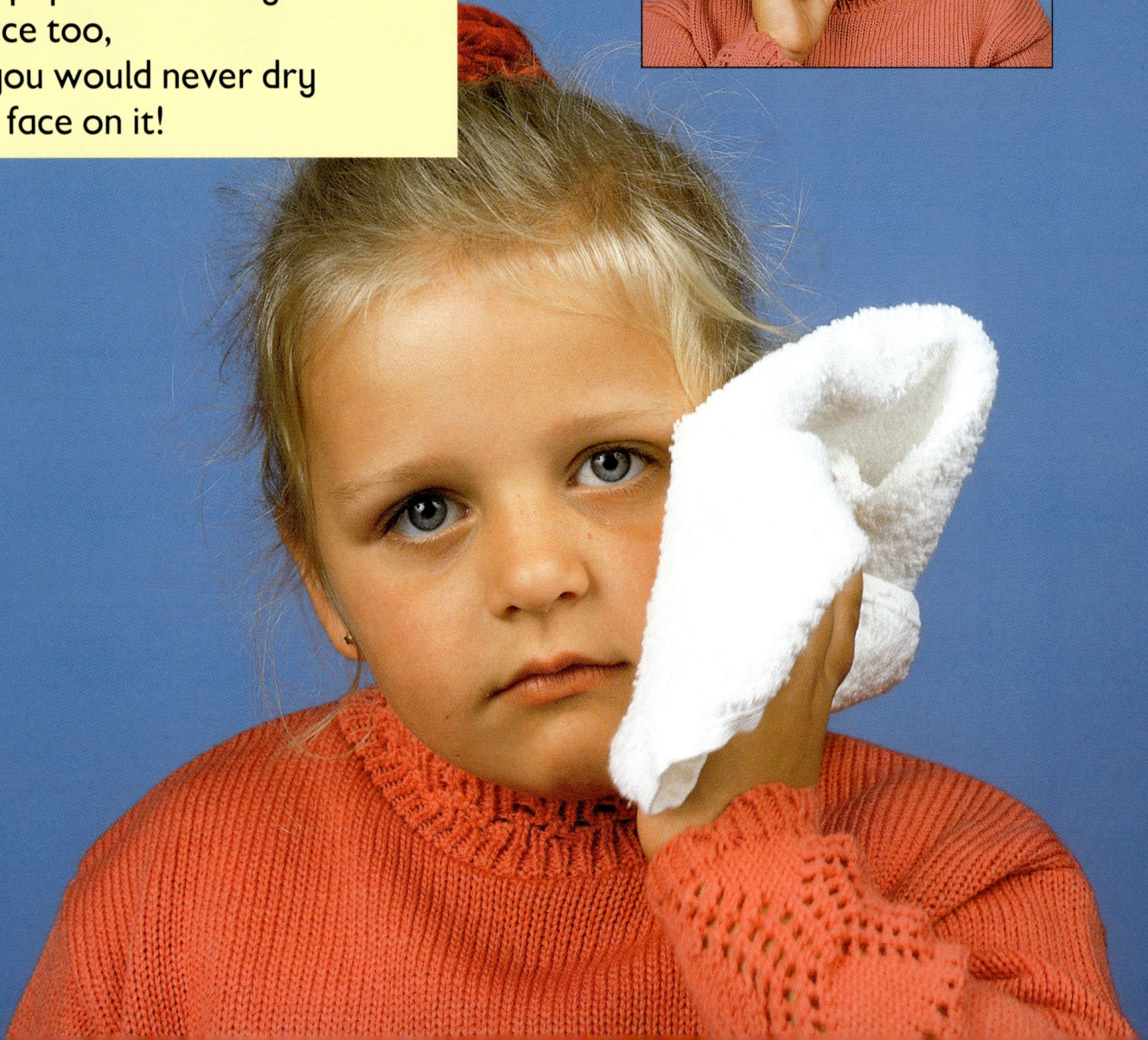

We can see and touch
the textures of the things
around us.
Some textures we can taste…
the roughness of crusty bread,
the smoothness of cream.

We cover our skins
with clothing.
Clothes have texture.

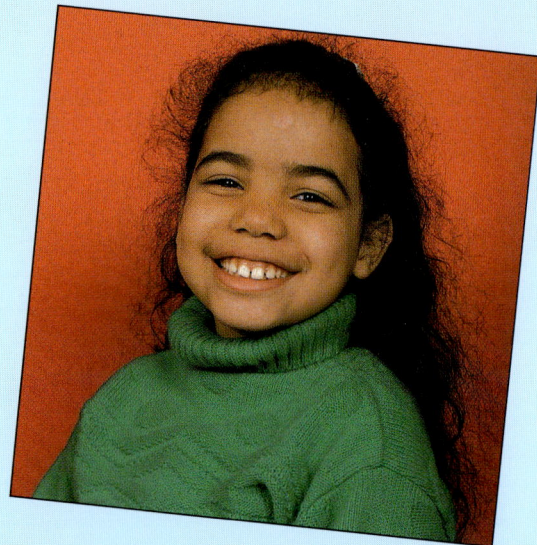

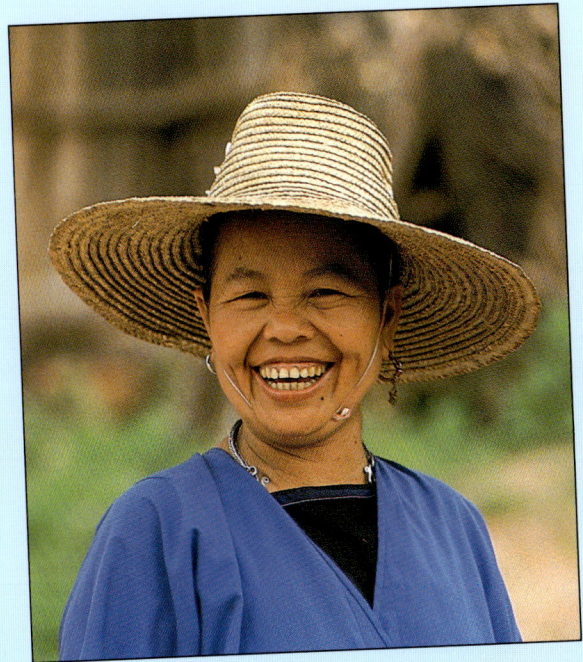

The texture of the clothes
we wear
helps keep us dry,
or cool
or warm.

How does the texture of the oil skin help keep this fisherman dry?

Texture can help us
do things more easily.
What are these used for?
How does their texture help?

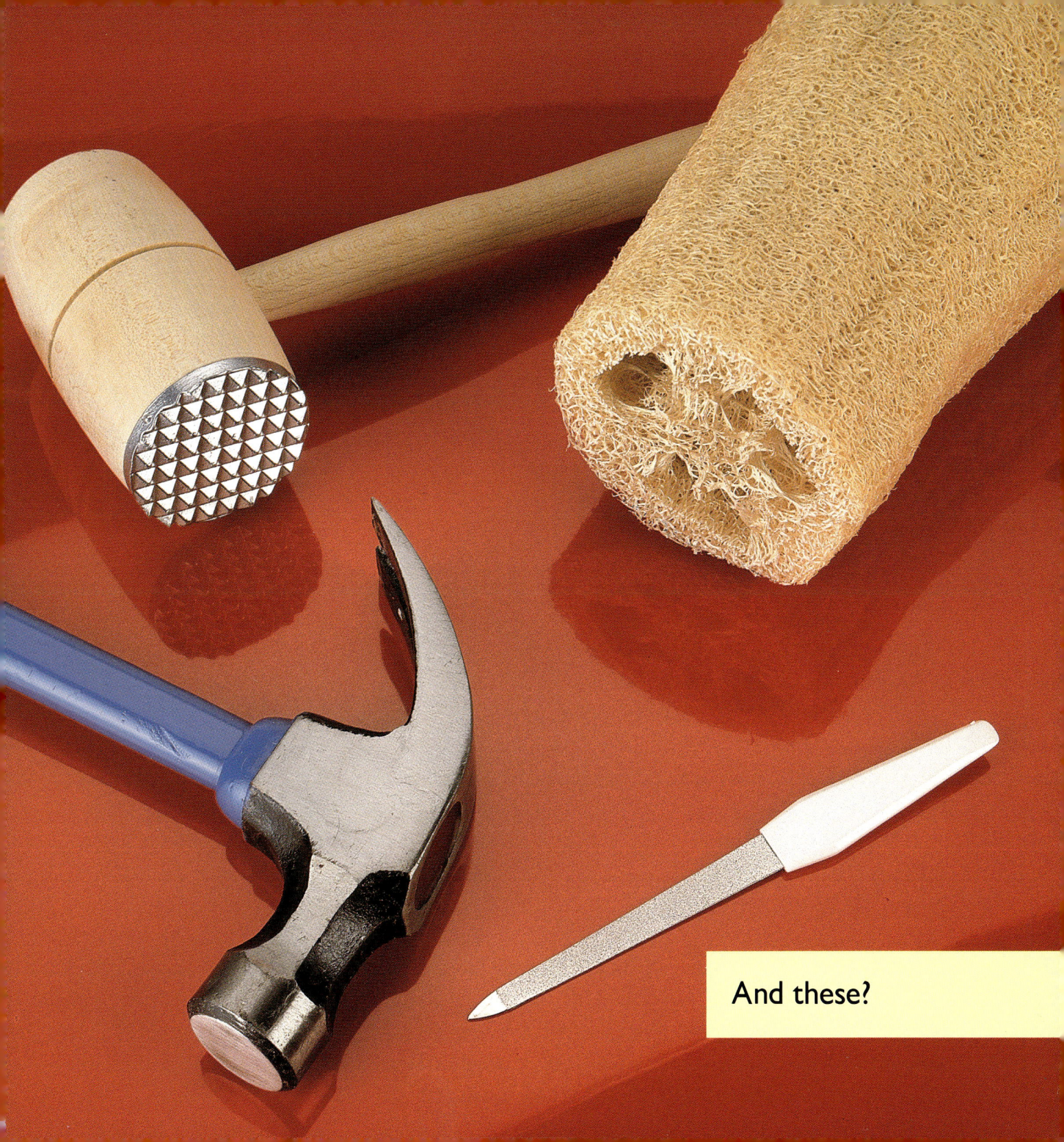

And these?

Texture is pattern
we can touch.
For people who cannot see
texture is very important.
Through textures like this
they can read.

Texture is an important
part of our lives.
Do you have
a favourite texture?

About this book

All books which are specially prepared for young children are written to meet the interest of the age group at which they are directed. This may mean presenting an idea in a humorous or unconventional way so that ideas which hitherto have been grasped somewhat hazily are given sharper focus. The books in this series aim to bring into focus some of the elements of life and living which we as adults tend to take for granted.

This book develops and explores an idea using simple text and thought-provoking photographs. The words will encourage questioning and discussion – whether they are read by adult or child. Children enjoy having information books read to them just as much as stories and poetry. The younger child may ignore the written words … pictures play an important part in learning, particularly if they encourage talk and visual discrimination.

Young children acquire much information in an incidental, almost random fashion. Indeed, they learn much just by being alive! The adult who uses books like this one needs to be sympathetic and understanding of the young child's intellectual development.
It offers a particular way of looking, an approach to questioning which will result in talk, rather than 'correct' one word answers.

Henry Pluckrose